## DATE DUE

| | |
|---|---|
| | |
| | |
| | |
| | |
| | |
| | |
| | |
| | |
| | |
| | |
| | |
| | |
| | |
| | |
| | |
| | |
| | |
| | |
| | |
| | PRINTED IN U.S.A. |

# JOSÉ BAUTISTA

## THE RISE TO THE TOP!

Bats in the Home Run Derby, and wins the Silver Slugger Award and the Hank Aaron Award for the second time.

## 2011

Plays in the All-Star Game and wins the title of Player of the Month for two months. Also wins the Silver Slugger Award, the MVP Award for his team, and the Hank Aaron Award.

## 2010

Starts to play for the Toronto Blue Jays.

## 2008

Signs with the Pittsburgh Pirates.

## 2000

Goes to school in the United States.

## 1998

Born in Santo Domingo.

## 1980

Mason Crest
370 Reed Road
Broomall, Pennsylvania 19008
www.masoncrest.com

Printed and bound in the United States of America.

First printing
9 8 7 6 5 4 3 2 1

Library of Congress Cataloging-in-Publication Data

Rodríguez Gonzalez, Tania.
  José Bautista / by Tania Rodriguez.
    p. cm.
  Includes index.
  ISBN 978-1-4222-2685-8 (hardcover) -- ISBN 978-1-4222-2670-4 (series hardcover) -- ISBN 978-1-4222-9174-0 (ebook)
  1.  Bautista, José, 1980---Juvenile literature. 2.  Hispanic American baseball players--Biography--Juvenile literature. 3.  Baseball players--United States--Biography--Juvenile literature.  I. Title.
  GV865.B325R64 2012
  796.357092--dc23
  [B]
                                                2012020944

Produced by Harding House Publishing Services, Inc.
www.hardinghousepages.com

Picture Credits:
Adam Jones: p. 6
Baseball Digest, page 19, December 1960 issue: p. 22
Keith Allison: p. 1, 8, 24
Mangin, Brad: p. 2, 10, 12, 14, 17, 18, 19, 25, 26, 28
Paul McKinnon | Dreamstime.com: p. 4

# JOSÉ BAUTISTA

## Chapter 1

# BASEBALL, THE DOMINICAN REPUBLIC, AND JOSÉ BAUTISTA

José Bautista hasn't been in baseball very long. But he's already made a name for himself in the sport. Bautista has already done things in baseball that many players can only dream of doing. He's played in the *All-Star Game* twice. He's hit more than 50 home runs in one season. He's won awards and made millions of dollars. Bautista is living his dream of playing baseball in *Major League Baseball (MLB)*.

*Dominican boys like these dream of one day being Major League baseball stars.*

Today, Bautista is one of baseball's newest stars. Bautista worked hard to get where he is now. His path to playing in the Majors began in his hometown, Santo Domingo in the Dominican Republic. As a boy growing up on the island, José was surrounded by a rich baseball culture. His culture helped him become the player he is today.

## The History of Dominican Baseball

Historians aren't exactly sure how baseball first came to the island, but they know it's been there since at least 1880.

Americans brought the game of baseball to the Caribbean in the mid-1860s when U.S. business interests grew in Cuba, one of the Dominican Republic's neighbors. Then, between 1868 and 1878, many Cubans fled their country during the Ten Years' War. Many of them ended up in the Dominican Republic. They brought the game of baseball with them—and it caught on fast!

The first Dominican baseball teams were formed either in the year 1894 or 1895. Eventually, strong teams took shape. These became the oldest baseball organizations in the country. They were the roots that grew into a thriving baseball culture.

Los Tigres de Licey was founded in Santo Domingo in 1907, and Las Estrellas Orientales was founded in San Pedro in 1911. By 1921, Licey had become so strong that three other teams decided to work together to defeat the Tigres. Los Muchachos, San Carlos, and Delco Light picked out their best players for a new team that would be powerful enough to beat Licey. They called their team Los Leones de Escogido. That same year, Sandino was also founded. Sandino was later renamed Las Águilas Cibaeñas in 1936.

Baseball fever spread across the island. Dominicans loved baseball! By the 1920s, teams from the Dominican Republic were playing other Caribbean nations. They also played teams from the United States. But all these games took place during the day, never at night—because the baseball fields in the Dominican Republic didn't have lights.

Then, in 1930, Rafael Leonidas Trujillo took control of the Dominican Republic. Trujillo controlled *everything* in the Dominican Republic—including baseball. He wanted his island to become a modern nation, so he made sure Dominican baseball was modern too. In 1955, he built the first major baseball stadium in the Dominican Republic, El

Estadio Trujillo, which later became Quisqueya Stadium. The stadium was well designed—and well lit as well! Now games could be played at night.

Trujillo helped baseball become his country's national pastime. Baseball was here to stay! The Golden Era of Dominican baseball had begun.

Players from the United States, especially from the Negro Leagues, came to play the Dominican Republic's finest players. The competition was fierce!

Today, the strength of Dominican baseball is found in each of the Major League's 30 teams. And at the same time, baseball is still just as popular on the island. José Bautista and all the other Dominican players in the Majors inspire boys playing ball in the streets of the Dominican Republic. These boys dream about being the next A-Rod . . . or maybe the next José Bautista.

Players like Bautista make their country proud. They prove that dreams can come true. But they also show that it takes hard work and talent to rise to the top of the game. José Bautista had to travel a long road before he became the player he is today.

## Early Life

José Bautista was born on October 19, 1980, in Santo Domingo, in the

*Bautista played for a lot of teams before he ended up with the Blue Jays.*

### Dominican Coaches and Managers

Dominicans are leaving their mark on other aspects of the game as well. In 2003, Tony Peña, who once played for the Kansas City Royals, coached against Felipe Alou, of the San Francisco Giants, making it the first time that two Dominicans coached against each other in the Major Leagues. And then, in 2004, Omar Minaya became the first Dominican General Manager, working the front office for the New York Mets. Dominicans are first-class leaders in the world of baseball!

Dominican Republic. He grew up in a town outside Santo Domingo called Baní.

José's father's name was Américo. His mother's name was Sandra. Américo helped to run a farm. Sandra worked as an accountant. José often helped his father around the farm.

José's parents worked hard to send José to a private school—and José worked hard to get good grades, too. He was smart and did well in school. José's parents always pushed him to do his best.

Growing up, José loved sports, especially baseball. But he wasn't the best player. José was fast, though. He could also catch well. José and his friends also played basketball and other sports.

As José got older, he got better and better at baseball. José had been skinny when he was young, but as he grew up,

he got bigger and stronger. Soon, José was playing baseball more than any other sport. And scouts from the United States were taking notice. Some scouts wanted to sign José. But he was going to take a different path.

When he was 18, José decided to go to college in the United States. He started going to Chipola Junior College in Florida. There, José played for the college's baseball team. José played very well, too. In 2000, José had an amazing season at Chipola.

Scouts from the Pittsburgh Pirates saw that José could be a great player. The Pirates *drafted* José after the 2000 season. José finally had his chance to play baseball for a living. He'd worked hard to go from the Dominican Republic to playing at college in Florida. But his hard work was about to pay off. José was on his way to the *minor leagues*.

## Chapter 2

# BAUTISTA BREAKS INTO BASEBALL

José Bautista began his career in baseball in 2001. The Pirates had Bautista play for one of the team's farm teams. Bautista would have to work his way up to playing for the Pittsburgh Pirates.

## Starting in the Minor Leagues

In 2001, Bautista played for the Williamsport Crosscutters. The Crosscutters are from Williamsport, Pennsylvania. The team plays in the New York-Pennsylvania League.

Bautista played in 62 games for Williamsport. During the 2001 season, he scored 43 runs and had 30 *runs batted in (RBIs)*. Bautista's batting percentage was .286 in 2001. On defense, Bautista mostly played third base. He also played a few games in the outfield.

In 2002, the Pirates moved Bautista to the Hickory Crawdads. The Crawdads are from Hickory, North Carolina. The team is part of the South Atlantic League. The team change didn't slow Bautista down at all. He played in more games than he did the year before. He also played much better.

Bautista played in 129 games for the Crawdads. During that time, he hit 14 home runs. He scored 72 runs and had 57 RBIs in 2002. Bautista's *batting average* was .301. Bautista played third base for most of the season. He also played shortstop for 2 games. His fielding percentage was .916 on third base. He also helped to make 12 *double plays*.

In the 2003 season, Bautista played for two teams. He started the season in the Gulf Coast League with the Pirates.

After a few games, he moved to the Lynchburg (Pennsylvania) Hillcats. Bautista was hurt in his fifty-first game with the Hillcats in 2003, though. He had to sit out for two months with a broken hand. When he came back to the team, he played for the Hillcats in the Carolina League *playoffs*.

## Bautista's Strange Year

Late in 2003, the Baltimore Orioles drafted Bautista. Bautista would be headed to play in Baltimore. He'd finally get his chance to play on a Major League team, even if it wasn't the Pirates.

Bautista started the 2003 season with the Orioles. He played backup third base. Bautista only played 16 games with the team, though. After that, the Orioles let him leave the team before his contract was up.

The Tampa Bay Rays *signed* Bautista not long after he left the Orioles. Bautista played in 12 games for the Rays. After that, the team sold Bautista to the Kansas City Royals. Bautista played just 13 games for the Royals before moving again. This time, Bautista joined the New York Mets.

Before he even played a game for the team, though, he was sent off to Pittsburgh again. The Mets had *traded*

*Bautista started his career with the Pirates, and then played for them again in 2004.*

## The Minor Leagues

Most baseball players don't go right from school to the Major Leagues. It's usually better when they can get some practice in the minor leagues first. The minor leagues operate in a bunch of countries, including Puerto Rico, the United States, Canada, Mexico, and the Dominican Republic.

Minor league teams form relationships with Major League teams. The Major Leagues look at the minor league players and decide who could play on their team. Sometimes the minor league teams are called "farm" teams. They "grow" players for the team they're connected to. Some of the relationships last a long time and some only last a couple years.

him to the Pirates. Bautista was back at the team he started on. Bautista finished the 2004 season playing with the Pirates in 23 games.

The 2004 season had been very strange for Bautista. He'd been with five teams in 2004. No other player in the MLB had ever had a year like Bautista's. Bautista didn't mind, though. He was back with the Pirates. He'd also been able to play in the Majors. Soon, he'd get the chance to play a lot more, too.

## Chapter 3

# PLAYING IN PITTSBURGH

I n 2005, the Pirates sent Bautista to play for the
Class AA Altoona Curve. The Curve play in
Altoona, Pennsylvania. The team is part of the
Eastern League. Bautista was back in the minors. But
he would make the most of it. And soon, he'd be
back in the Majors.

## A Step Back

In the 2005 season, Bautista played in 117 games for the Curve. While playing for Altoona, Bautista scored 63 runs. He had 90 RBIs and hit 23 home runs. Bautista's batting average was .283 while playing for the Curve.

Bautista played well enough for the Pirates to move him to a Class AAA team. Bautista played in 13 games for the Indianapolis Indians in 2005.

After playing with the Indians, Bautista got his chance to play in the Majors again. The Pirates brought Bautista up from the minors to play in 11 games at the end of the 2005 season.

## Playing for the Pirates

In 2006, Bautista began the season with the Indianapolis Indians. But he only played in 29 games for the team before going back to the Pirates. Bautista spent the rest of the year playing in the Majors. He played in 117 games for the Pirates. He scored 58 runs and had 51 RBIs. Bautista hit 16 home runs for the Pirates in 2006. His batting average was .235.

Bautista played many different positions on the Pirates' *defense*. He played second and third base. He played right, left, and center field. Bautista spent the most time in center field. He started at

center field in 46 games in 2006. His fielding percentage while playing center field was .984 in 57 games.

In the 2007 season, Bautista played in 142 games for the Pirates. At first, he played many positions like he did in 2006. But soon, the Pirates made Bautista their starting third baseman. Bautista started at third in 122 games in 2007. His fielding percentage at third base was .958.

At bat, Bautista did about as well as he had in 2006. He hit 15 home runs during the 2007 season. Bautista scored 75 runs and had 63 RBIs. His batting average for the season was .254.

The Pirates didn't have a very good season in 2007, though. The team finished the season with a losing record. The Pirates had won 68 games and lost 94. The team finished last in the National League Central *division*.

## Traded to Toronto

The next year, Bautista began the season playing third base for the Pirates. He played in 107 games for Pittsburgh. In that time, Bautista scored 38 runs and had 44 RBIs. His batting average was .242. Bautista started at third base in 81 games for the Pirates. But soon, the Pirates moved Bautista to back-up third base.

**15**

JOSE Bautista
PITTSBURGH PIRATES® 3rd BASE

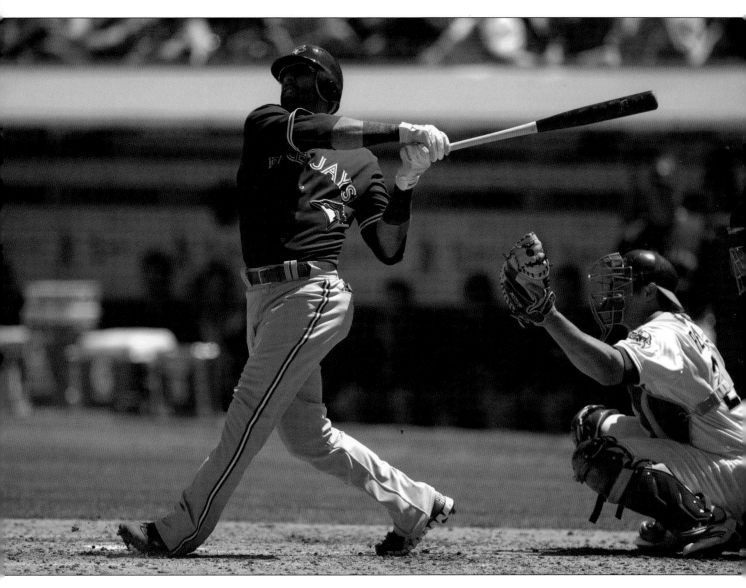

*Bautista was happy to be with the Blue Jays, and the Blue Jays were happy to have him on the team.*

Not long after that, Bautista was moved from the Pirates back to the minors. Pittsburgh sent Bautista to play with the Indianapolis Indians again. After just five games, Bautista was traded to the Toronto Blue Jays. He was leaving the Pirates again. But this was the chance he needed to play in the Majors again.

Bautista finished the 2008 season playing for Toronto. He played in 21 games for the Blue Jays. Bautista had another year of moving between teams. But now that he'd been traded to Toronto, he'd get a chance to stay with one team for a while.

## Chapter 4

# BAUTISTA WITH THE BLUE JAYS

Bautista played many positions for the Toronto Blue Jays in 2009. Bautista was used to changes, though. He'd spent a lot of time playing different positions with the Pirates, as well. Bautista played at third base for the Blue Jays. He also played left, right, and center field.

At the beginning of the 2009 season, Bautista didn't play much. He was on the bench, ready to take over for Toronto's starting third baseman if he had to. But soon, Bautista was playing more and more. He became the Blue Jays' leadoff hitter and got better at bat.

Bautista finished the season with 13 home runs. He hit 10 home runs in September alone. Bautista also had 40 RBIs and scored 54 runs. Bautista's batting average was .235 in 2009. On defense, Bautista played well. He played in left field more than any other position. There, his fielding percentage was .984.

*The Blue Jays saw Bautista's potential.*

The Blue Jays didn't have their best season in 2009. The team finished with a losing record. The Blue Jays won 75 games and lost 87 in 2009. The team finished fourth in the American League East division.

After the 2009 season, the Blue Jays gave Bautista a new contract. He agreed to play one more season for the Blue Jays—and the team agreed to pay Bautista $2.4 million dollars to play for Toronto in 2010.

## A Big Year

The 2010 season was the biggest of Bautista's career in the Major Leagues. He had an amazing year. He played well and put up big numbers. He won awards and was able to do things many players can only dream about.

Bautista had finished the 2009 season very strong. He hit 10 home runs in just one month at the end of the season. In 2010, Bautista wanted to keep hitting as well. At the start of the season, he didn't do as well as he wanted to. But in May, Bautista hit 12 home runs. He also won the American League Player of the Week award in mid-May. By the middle of June, Bautista had hit 20 home runs.

In July, Bautista was chosen to play in the ***All-Star Game***. The game was Bautista's first All-Star Game, but it wouldn't be his last. At the end of the month, Bautista hit his 30th home run of the season. He had hit 11 home runs in July alone. Bautista won the American League Player of the Month for July 2010.

Bautista won the award again in August, as well. No player in the American League hit more home runs than Bautista. No AL player had more RBIs either.

Bautista didn't slow down in September. In a game on September 23, Bautista hit his 50th home run of the 2010 season. Before Bautista, only 25 players had hit 50 homers in one year.

Bautista finished the season with 54 home runs. He scored 109 runs and had 124 RBIs in 2010. Bautista's batting average was .260. On defense, he played many positions. But he played at third base and in right field most often. Bautista started at right field in 113 games. His fielding percentage in the position was .985.

The Blue Jays 2010 season wasn't as amazing as Bautista's, but the team finished with a better record than it had in 2009. The Blue Jays won 85 games and lost 77. Still, the team finished just fourth in their division.

### Hank Aaron

One of the best baseball players of all time was Hank Aaron. He was born in Alabama in 1934. Because he was black, he had to play in the Negro Leagues when he started out. Back then, baseball was segregated. Black people and white people couldn't play together. Aaron was a big deal in the Negro Leagues. He helped his team win the league's World Series. He was so good that the MLB noticed him. In 1953, the Milwaukee Braves (today the Atlanta Braves) signed him on. Later he played for the Milwaukee Brewers.

Aaron holds a lot of records. He has 2,297 RBIs and has hit 755 homeruns during his career. In recent years, that record has been broken. But Hank Aaron lives on in the memories and imaginations of baseball fans everywhere.

*Hank Aaron*

At the end of the 2010 season, Bautista was given many awards. He was given the Silver Slugger Award. The Blue Jays named Bautista the team's *Most Valuable Player (MVP)*. He also won the American League Hank Aaron Award.

Bautista had turned his career around and achieved a lot in just one year. He'd played well and won many awards. Fans watched him break records and hit homer after homer. Bautista wanted to make sure that he played just as well in 2011. And he was ready to work hard to make it happen.

## Chapter 5

# JOSÉ BAUTISTA TODAY

In early 2011, the Blue Jays and Bautista agreed to a new contract. Bautista agreed to play for the Blue Jays for five seasons. The team would pay Bautista $64 million over five years. Bautista started the 2011 season as Toronto's starting right fielder. And 2011 would be yet another big year for Bautista.

## Another Great Season

In April 2011, Bautista had a great start to the season. He hit 9 home runs in April. Bautista was named American League Player of the Month. In May, Bautista kept playing well. By the end of the month, he'd hit 20 home runs. No other player had as many homers at that point in the season. Bautista won the American League Player of the Month award again in May.

In June, Bautista started playing third base for the Blue Jays. He was also chosen to play in the All-Star Game. No other player had ever gotten more votes to play in the All-Star Game from baseball fans. Bautista got more than 7.4 million votes. Bautista also got a chance to join in the Home Run Derby in 2011.

*Finally, Bautista could shine with the Blue Jays.*

*Bautista takes a great swing!*

Bautista played very well for the rest of the season. By early September, he'd already hit 40 home runs. By the end of the season, Bautista hit 43 home runs. He had scored 105 runs and had 103 RBIs. Bautista's batting average was .302 in 2011.

At the end of the 2011 season, Bautista won the Silver Slugger Award. He also won the American League Hank Aaron Award for the second time. Only two other players have won the award two years in a row.

The Blue Jays didn't have an amazing season, but the team could have done worse, too. The Blue Jays finished the 2011 season with 81 wins and 81 losses. The team placed fourth in the American League East. Still, Bautista had another big season. The Blue Jays' star was a favorite of fans in Toronto. Fans hoped Bautista would lead the team to win more games and even make it to the post-season in 2012.

## What's Next?

Baseball fans know José Bautista for his big swing. They know him for the awards he's won and the numbers he's put up. Bautista has played very well in the last few years. He has become one of base-ball's newest stars. Not many players can hit 50 home runs in one year! Not many players have won the Hank Aaron award twice in two years either! Bautista has proven that he's a great player. Few other players could hope to do the things that Bautista has done.

Bautista has a lot more to do in base-ball, too. He hasn't won a World Series, yet. He hasn't even played in a post-season game! Bautista may have big numbers and big hits, but he still has goals to reach in baseball.

Bautista worked hard to make it into the Majors. He worked his way through the minor leagues. He even had to go back to the minors after playing in the big leagues. But no matter what, Bautista kept going. He kept working hard to reach his dream of playing baseball in the Majors. And today, he's living that dream. His journey from the Dominican Republic to the Toronto Blue Jays was a long one. But all of Bautista's hard work has paid off.

No one can say what's next for Bautista. But one thing is for sure. He won't stop working hard to reach his goals. He won't stop trying his best to succeed.

*Bautista has a lot left to give to baseball.*

# Find Out More

## *Online*

**Baseball Almanac**

www.baseball-almanac.com

**Baseball Hall of Fame**

baseballhall.org

**Baseball Reference**

www.baseball-reference.com

**Dominican Baseball**

mlb.mlb.com/mlb/features/dr/

index.jsp

**History of Baseball**

www.19cbaseball.com

**Major League Baseball**

www.mlb.com

**Science of Baseball**

www.exploratorium.edu/baseball

# Index